TOP 10 WAYS
ACCIDENT VICTIMS
SABOTAGE
THEIR OWN CASE

BY JACOB JOHNSTUN
ART GEDIMIN A. BULAT

Copyright © 2016 by Jacob Johnstun

Printed in the United States of America

ISBN-13: 978-1535146814
ISBN-10: 1535146818

First Printing, 2016

Johnstun Injury Law
P.O. Box 1660
St. Helens, OR 97051

Phone: (503)610-5399
Fax: (866)955-2236
johnstun.injury.law@outlook.com

Art by Gedimin A Bulat, www.gedimin.com

Contents

Your own worst enemy.

Introduction

Have you ever thought you were making something better, but all you ended up doing was making things worse? If you're human, then of course you have. I have too. Just ask my wife! But when it comes to your personal injury case, it is not the time to be making mistakes. Depending on the seriousness of your injuries, the stakes can be high, and the margin for error small. One misstep could be the difference between a fair settlement that will get you back on your feet and getting absolutely nothing.

That's why I wrote this book. I've seen too many people become their own worst enemy and sabotage their case, simply because they didn't have an easy way to learn what they should and should not do. You and other accident victims deserve to have some kind of map, written in plain English, telling you where certain pitfalls are and how to avoid them. That way, you'll know exactly how to help yourself and your case, and not just make things worse.

I've written this with mostly car accident victims in mind, since they're by far the most common type of accident victims. But, if you've been injured and it was somebody else's fault, whether it was due to a bicycle accident, dangerous and defective product, dog attack, etc., many of the same lessons apply to you. So take some time to skim through this book. It just might save your case.

Legal Disclaimer

This book is presented solely for educational purposes. The author and publisher are not offering it as legal advice. While best efforts have been used in preparing this book, the author and publisher make no representations or warranties of any kind and assume no liabilities of any kind with respect to the accuracy or completeness of the contents and specifically disclaim any implied warranties of merchantability or fitness of use for a particular purpose. Neither the author nor the publisher shall be held liable or responsible to any person or entity with respect to any loss or incidental or consequential damages caused, or alleged to have been caused, directly or indirectly, by the information contained herein. Every personal injury case is different and the advice and strategies contained herein may not be suitable for your situation. You should seek the services of a competent attorney for any legal questions you might have.

SELF-SABOTAGE #1

Believing The Car Insurance Company Is Your Friend

*Getting a fair settlement from the insurance company can be like trying to take a banana from a monkey. A really, really **big** monkey.*

My wife Dawn and I recently went to a home and garden show with our six month old son, Jess (named after his grandpa). We walked around the showroom slowly, commenting on the things we liked and didn't like, while I pushed our son's stroller awkwardly because the handlebars seem to have been designed for parents less than five feet tall. We were eventually stopped by a vendor who was selling dishwashers. He told us all about the dishwasher's incredible features and the problems it would solve. If we were seriously in the market for buying a new dishwasher (which we weren't), we would have told the salesman that we would think about his product, slipped away out of sight, and have done some quick research on our phones to check out the customer satisfaction ratings of this particular dishwasher. Why would we do that? Why wouldn't we just take the salesman at his word?

I'm willing to bet you know the answer, because you've reacted the same way many times before. You know the salesman's main goal is to make the sale, so he has an incentive to overstate how incredible that dishwasher really is. In order to protect yourself from this sort of thing, you probably drink a healthy dose of skepticism every morning before leaving the house. Some of you may even drink two for good measure.

What does this have to do with your car accident? Well, I've used this example to illustrate your relationship with the insurance company. Would you say the salesman above was my friend?   Should I call him my "good neighbor?" Or how about a "Good Samaritan" that will hold my hand through the hard times?   Of course you wouldn't.   It was just business, that's all.   Your relationship with an insurance company is no different.

Here's how it works: You pay a premium, an amount of money, every six months or so to the insurance company, and in exchange it agrees to pay for specific bad events in your life, like death, fire, or accident.   The insurance company makes this deal with you because it is betting that, in the long run, you will have to pay it more than it will have to pay you.   It's right most of the time.   But when it's wrong, and bad events do happen, the insurance company will attempt to minimize what it pays out.   It is not friendship.   It is not personal.   It's just business.

Many are confused about the nature of this relationship (kind of like the female contestants on The Bachelor who tell the audience "We're in love!" even though he's getting cozy with a different girl in the next room).   And it's no wonder why.   Every year, insurance companies spend billions of dollars on advertising.   Geico alone spent $1.18 billion in 2013.   Insurance ads are often filled with warm, friendly slogans and feel-good music playing in the background.   You probably know these ones by heart:

"You're in good hands with Allstate."

"Like a good neighbor, State Farm is there."

"Nationwide is on your side."

They go to great lengths to convince you they are something they are not: your friend. I can't help but think of a certain expression when I see some of their marketing campaigns…

You can put lipstick on a pig, but it's still a pig.

I've explained the dynamics of this relationship because it can be a dangerous thing to misunderstand. Think back to our dishwasher salesman. We all know it's a common practice among salespeople to quote a higher price for their product at first, and then gradually reduce the price through haggling and negotiating until they get to a figure that's agreeable to both parties. Undoubtedly, the salesperson will sell his product for the highest price he can. So if I mistakenly believed that the salesman was my friend, I wouldn't have seen a need to haggle with him. Instead, I would have foolishly trusted him to automatically give me the best deal he could from the start. This would have caused me to hastily accept the first offer quoted by him, and I'd be stuck paying sticker price when I could have paid much less.

Insurance companies employ very similar tactics. It is the normal, common practice to only give accident victims lowball and inadequate offers at first. Then, they gradually increase their offers if the victims, or their attorneys, can show that the law requires them to pay more. They rarely offer a fair settlement upfront. And this makes sense, at least from a business perspective, doesn't it? The goal of any business is to be more profitable, and the less money they have to give you to settle your claim, the better it is for them. So if an accident victim mistakenly believes the insurance company is his friend, while their relationship is actually adversarial, things are not going to end well. Just imagine

When dealing with the insurance company, it's best to keep your guard up.

what would happen if a boxer thought the guy across the ring was his teammate!

I think it's insane how adversarial this whole process is. If someone does harm to you or your property, the right thing for him to do would be to take responsibility for what he has done and compensate you for it, right? So why should it be any different when somebody slams into you with their car? If you need a doctor, or physical therapy, or acupuncture, the at-fault driver and his insurance company should offer to pay for all of it. If you're too hurt to go to work for a period of time, they should offer to pay for that too. You shouldn't have to fight for it. Unfortunately, the system isn't set up that way. At least now, you know there's a fight going on and who you're fighting against, and you won't be lured into a false sense of security with those who don't have your best interests at heart.

Don't expect the insurance company to just take your word for it.

L et's say you're taking a little stroll in downtown Portland. A man you've never seen before approaches you, claiming you owe him money. "What for?" you ask. He answers "A few weeks ago, I noticed a parking ticket on the windshield of your car, so I took it and paid it for you." I doubt you would automatically believe his story. Surely you would ask him for some kind of proof, such as the original ticket or the receipt he got when he (supposedly) made this payment on your behalf. And if he had no proof, then despite all the excuses he might make, I imagine you would respond "I'm sorry, but I don't know you, and if you can't prove to me that what you're saying is true, I can't help you."

I think this serves as a good example because, if your accident was someone else's fault, either you or your attorney will eventually tell their insurance company it owes you money. Naturally, the insurance company is going to want you to prove it. One type of proof it will expect is a Traffic Accident Report from a police officer. This report will show that there was indeed an accident, who was involved, who was at fault, and whether any citations were written. Once an officer creates a Traffic Accident Report that says this whole thing was the other guy's fault, it makes it very difficult for his insurance company to deny it owes you at least something. But if the police are not called, and no Traffic Accident Report exists, it is easier for the insurance company to tell you "We're sorry, but we don't know you, and if you can't prove to us that what you're saying is true, we can't help you."

I doubt this mistake would be fatal to your case if you've made it already. There are a lot of other ways to prove there was an accident and that it was the other guy's fault. There might be witnesses who will confirm your version of the story. Or, if you were rear-ended, it almost automatically means the other driver was at fault because he was following too closely or not paying attention. And these are just for starters.

SELF-SABOTAGE #3

Forgetting To Gather Evidence

Gathering evidence from the accident scene can go a long way in helping your case.

I get it. The last thing you're doing right after a serious car accident is thinking clearly. I know from personal experience. While driving home from work in summer 2015, my car hydroplaned and crashed going 60 mph (I wasn't speeding, in case you're curious). I had a serious concussion. Even though I was handling personal injury cases every day, my head was so foggy that I couldn't remember what to do. So if your head isn't working right like mine wasn't, or you're just too hurt to walk around, that's alright. Don't worry about it. But, if you are able, it is a good idea to put on your detective hat and collect evidence by doing the following:

✓ **Take lots of pictures. You'll want photos of:**

- You and your passengers' visible injuries;
- The damage to your car;
- The damage to the other person's car (be polite and get their permission first);
- Any debris that the accident caused;
- The accident scene; and...
- Anything else you think might be relevant.

✓ **If you talk to the other driver, write down your conversation that same day!**

✓ **Make sure either you or the responding police officer gets the other driver's contact and insurance information.**

✓ **If there are witnesses, ask them for their contact information. Also ask if they could give you a signed statement, or, if they prefer, use an app on your phone to record a verbal statement.**

✓ **Write down everything you remember about the accident as soon as you can. If you wait too long, it gives the insurance company room to argue that your memory has faded over time.**

Above all, be safe! There might be a lot of traffic around you, so don't do anything until you get you and your passengers out of harm's way first.

SELF-SABOTAGE #4

Neglecting Your Medical Care

Brian's being stubborn. Don't be like Brian.

TOUGHING IT OUT

This is one of the more serious mistakes I've seen people make. Quite often, car accident victims underestimate how traumatic their injuries really are, so they decide not to seek treatment. I've given an imaginary, yet typical example below to show how foolish of a decision this can be:

On his way to karate practice, Brian gets rear-ended at a stop sign. Brian soon realizes he's suffered whiplash and a concussion. He thinks to himself "I'm a tough karate guy! I have a black belt, for crying out loud! I don't need any stinkin' doctors!"

Over the next several weeks, Brian is forced to skip karate practice because his injuries aren't getting better. They're getting worse. His wife sees how miserable he is and tells him to see their doctor. But Brian is stubborn, and he ignores her.

Two months go by since Brian's accident. Finally, after being in pain for so long, Brian admits defeat and sees his doctor. The doctor says "Gee, Brian. I really wish you had seen me right away after your accident. I could have shortened your recovery time by a lot. Since you didn't, this whole experience is going to be much harder on you."

Brian starts to feel better after some physical therapy and acupuncture sessions. After receiving the bills for these treatments in the mail, Brian decides to call up the car insurance company so it will take care of them. "Hold on, Brian," the insurance adjuster tells him. "I'm afraid I have to deny your claim. From what I see, you didn't receive any treatment for over two months after the accident. You must not have been hurt. Otherwise, you would have seen a doctor sooner."

Panicking, Brian hastily explains that he really was hurt, but he made the mistake of trying to let his injuries heal on their own. "I'm sorry, Brian," the adjuster says, "but I don't believe you. There's no way that someone would wait that long before seeking treatment if they were really in that much pain. You could have fallen down some stairs last week, and are only saying it was the car accident that caused these injuries to get us to pay for your medical bills." (Claims are denied like this *all the time*.)

The moral of the story is this: Brian messed up. Don't be like Brian. His tough-guy attitude not only caused him more physical pain, but he's going to get less money too. Perhaps nothing. Fair or not, insurance companies assume that if you don't go to a doctor right after your accident, you must not have been hurt. Therefore, in their minds, any care that you get later on must have been caused by something else, and so they take the position that they don't have to pay. Don't give them this excuse. Go get the care you need, and fast.

QUITTING TOO EARLY

To illustrate another mistake people make, let's change Brian's story a little bit:

> After his car accident, Brian is smart and gets to a doctor right away. After just a few weeks of treatment, Brian notices he's beginning to feel much better. He asks his doctor "Hey doc, would it be alright if I didn't make any more appointments? They take up so much of my time, and I think I'm almost better anyway." His doctor responds "I'm glad you're feeling better, but I don't think you're ready to be discharged yet. Your neck and back are still really tense. You could be right back where you started if you stop treatment too early."

> Against medical advice, Brian stops his treatment. Months go by. But instead of Brian's injuries going away like he hoped they would, they get worse, just like his doctor predicted. Finally, Brian goes back to his doctor and admits he was wrong to have ever left in the first place (kind

of like what happens in every chick-flick movie ever). He starts to get better again.

Eventually, Brian calls up the car insurance company to have it pay for all of his treatment. The adjuster tells him "We can certainly take care of these first few medical bills of yours, Brian. Unfortunately, there's nothing we can do about the later ones. You see, when you stopped going to your doctor several months ago, you must have been all better. You wouldn't have stopped otherwise. And since you were all better, any medical care you get now will be unnecessary, and we don't pay for unnecessary medical care. So no, we can't pay for these new treatments you're getting." (This also happens *all the time.*)

Again, Brian messed up. Don't be like Brian. Like him, a lot of people get tired of medical treatment interrupting their schedules. That's why they sometimes decide to stop going before their treatment is completed. But no matter how inconvenient your doctor visits, physical therapy appointments, acupuncture or chiropractic sessions may be, resist this temptation! First and foremost, you would be forcing yourself to endure more physical pain than necessary. You stand a much better chance of being pain-free sooner if you see your treatment through to the end. Second, you would be lowering the value of your case, since the amount of your settlement partially depends on how much medical care you receive. Third, you would run the risk of eventually needing to go back to your doctor, only to be told by the insurance company that it won't pay for it, as was the case with Brian. So that comes out to at least three really bad things you would be doing to yourself if you quit treatment early, all for the sake of freeing up your schedule a little. It's just not worth it.

"BUT I CAN'T AFFORD IT"

Another reason why many accident victims decide to forego seeing a doctor is because they feel they can't afford it. This is a huge, huge mistake. In Oregon, your car insurance company is required to pay for at least the first $15,000 in medical care that you need. Your own policy might provide even more, depending on the amount of coverage you have. This section of your car insurance policy is called **Personal Injury Protection**, or PIP. Because of your PIP benefits, it doesn't matter how strapped you are for cash after a car accident. You can still get the medical care you need without having to personally worry about the first $15,000 in medical bills. And if the PIP funds become exhausted, your health insurance may be able to step in and take care of some or all of the bills after that. So you see, accident victims who avoid medical care because they feel they can't afford it are unnecessarily depriving themselves of insurance benefits which they have already paid for.

DO NOT DO THIS!

Soon after your car accident, the at-fault driver's insurance company is going to give you a call. Perhaps this has already happened. During your conversation, the adjuster is going to ask you something like "Mrs. Smith, could you tell me exactly what happened at the time of your car accident? And by the way, would it be alright with you if I recorded your statement for our records? I'm just trying to get everything resolved in the best way possible, and I would like to refer back to your statement if needed." DO NOT DO THIS. It will not help your case. It could only hurt it. The other guy's insurance company has its fingers crossed that you'll say something it can use against you.

For example, let's say the adjuster asks you a simple question like "How are you feeling?" Even though you're feeling crummy, you reply "Oh, I guess I'm feeling ok" because you're an optimist and you don't like to complain. Well, the adjuster could use this seemingly harmless dialogue to hurt your case. He'll argue "No, Mr. Johnstun. We can't pay for any more of your client's medical treatment because she told me she was feeling fine." I know this sounds ridiculous to you, and I couldn't agree more, but this happens! So it's best you avoid this whole mess completely and decline to give a recorded statement to the other guy's insurance company. In fact, it's best if you don't talk to them at all.

However, if it is your own insurance company that wants a recorded statement from you, it is a trickier situation. The difference here is that you have a policy, or contract, with your own insurance company. This policy/contract requires you to cooperate with its investigation. If your own insurance company insists that you give a recorded statement, you have three options. Your first option would be to hire an attorney who would be present while you gave a recorded statement. That way, if the adjuster were to ask you anything improper, your attorney could protect you from those questions.

Your second option would be to just go ahead and give the recorded statement on your own. But if you do this, be as factual in your statement as possible. By that, I mean only describe what you observed – just the facts. Don't talk about your thoughts, opinions, or feelings. And if you don't know the answer to something, say "I don't know," no matter how much they try to pressure you for a concrete answer. Don't try to guess!

Your third option would be to refuse giving a recorded statement. Be warned, however, that your adjuster could justifiably say "Alright Mr. Jones, if you won't help us, then according to the terms of your policy, we can close out your file and not pay you anything."

Clearly, option one would be ideal in this situation.

SELF-SABOTAGE #6

Accepting A Settlement Too Soon

Joey the klutz strikes again!

I understand you would like nothing more than to get all this behind you. I know you could really use any money the at-fault driver's insurance company is offering you, even if it's only a little. But let's put this in perspective, so that you don't panic and accept a lowball settlement.

Let's say you've gone out to dinner with a few friends. One of your friends, Joey, is, well, let's be honest, not the most coordinated person in the world. While reaching for the bread, Joey accidentally knocks over your drink, causing it to spill all over your cellphone. Unfortunately for you, your phone is not waterproof. You dry it off, but it won't turn on. "I'm really sorry," he says to you. "Could I pay for your meal to make it up to you?"

What would you do in this situation? Could you pass up a free meal? Or would you tell Joey "Thanks for the offer, but first let's wait until I find out how much it's going to cost to fix or replace my phone." Hopefully you would do the latter, because if it ends up costing $500 to fix or replace your phone, and you let Joey off the hook for $20, you'd be in the hole $480!

Your situation with the at-fault driver and his insurance company is no different. Like Joey, his insurance company will approach you with a low offer quickly, *before you could possibly know the full extent of the harm the accident has caused you.* Unless you have a crystal ball and can see the future, you don't know at this point how many doctor visits you'll need or what they'll cost; you don't know how many physical therapy/chiropractic/acupuncturist visits you'll need or what they'll cost; you don't know how much gas money you'll need to get to all of your medical appointments; and you don't know how this is going to affect your work and how much time you'll have to take off. So please, *please*, be patient, and wait until you're all better before even thinking about accepting a settlement offer. That way, you'll be able to find out how much this whole thing actually cost and what it's going to take for them to make things right. Besides, isn't that the whole point of insurance?

SELF-SABOTAGE #7

Posting On Social Media

Your friends aren't the only ones who might see your posts.

Just like Dale Carnegie said in his classic book *How to Win Friends and Influence People,* all of us want to feel important. We crave other people's recognition, and that craving is the driving force behind much of what we do. It's no wonder why we post so often on our social media accounts. When a high school girl posts a selfie after doing her makeup, she does it because she wants others to say "Wow, you look great!" Earlier today when one of my Facebook friends posted "If everyone knew everything, would we all have the same opinions? #AnesthesiaDeepThoughts," he did it because he wants other people to think "Haha, that guy is pretty funny, and smart too!" When I posted a picture of myself winning the Portland Highland Games' Kilted Mile years ago (flip to page 58 if you're curious), I admit I wanted others to think "Holy cow, that guy is fast!" If they thought I looked particularly dashing in a kilt, all the better. And when we post about the hard times we're going through, it's because we're looking for proof that other people care and that we matter. With this last point in mind, I'm still going to ask you to post nothing, and I mean *Nothing* with a capital "N," about your car accident.

Believe me, I know how traumatizing accidents can be. I know how much you could use all the support you can get right now, even if it's only a few words of encouragement from friends on Facebook. I hate to take that away from you. But if you listen to my advice, it could save your case, and here's why. ***The insurance company is going to look*** *up your social media accounts.* There aren't any "maybe's" or "probably's" about it. This is going to happen. When it does, the insurance company will look for anything it can use to hurt your claim.

Let's say you post something innocent like "Feeling much better today." If the insurance company were to see that, there's a good chance it would interpret your post to mean "I'm 100% better! So please, insurance company, don't pay for any more of my medical treatment because I don't need it." Of course, anyone with any sense at all would know you really meant "I'm not all better yet, but I'm making progress." But this is insurance we're talking about. It's not about common sense. It's about business.

Perhaps you're thinking "I appreciate your concern, Mr. Johnstun, but my Facebook account and Twitter feed can only be viewed by my friends, so there's nothing to worry about." While this is certainly an added protection, it's not bulletproof. If you or the attorney you hire cannot reach a fair agreement with the insurance company, your case will go to trial. Not long before trial, the insurance company could ask for copies of everything you've posted, and the judge might make you hand them over. No privacy setting is going to do you any good if that happens.

Here's what I'm not saying: I'm not saying to delete posts about your accident if you've made them already. The insurance company has ways of finding this stuff out. And if it sees that you've deleted posts relating to your accident, it could accuse you of destroying evidence. I'm sure I don't need to tell you how disastrous that could be for you. So if you haven't already posted anything about your case on social media, great! But if you have, then in the immortal words of The Beatles, I say "Let it be."

SELF-SABOTAGE #8

Not Hiring An Attorney

Sometimes a whole pie doesn't measure up to part of a much larger pie.

When injury victims decide not to hire an attorney, it's because of money most of the time. They find out, after some quick research, that most personal injury attorneys will take about a third of the final settlement as their fee. That's when they think "What?! A third?! That's crazy! I'll be better off figuring this out on my own. That way, I get to keep the whole pie." Being a frugal person myself, I think this is a very rational thought. And while it's true they would get to keep the whole pie, what they don't realize is that it would likely be a much smaller pie.

On average, injury victims who hire an attorney end up getting over three times as much money as those who don't.[1] That means that on average, those who use an attorney will take home over two times as much, even after paying legal fees. This makes sense, doesn't it? I would expect a chef to prepare a better meal, an artist to paint a better picture, and a musician to write a better song than I ever could. Hence, we should also expect an attorney to advocate for your cause better than a non-attorney.

So while not hiring an attorney might sound like the financially responsible thing to do at first, it's actually quite the opposite. You'd be shooting yourself in the foot.

---

[1] You can verify this by looking up the Insurance Research Counsel's 2014 report titled *Attorney Involvement in Auto Injury Claims.* Though there is a fee to access the report itself, there are plenty of online articles that discuss this portion of the report.

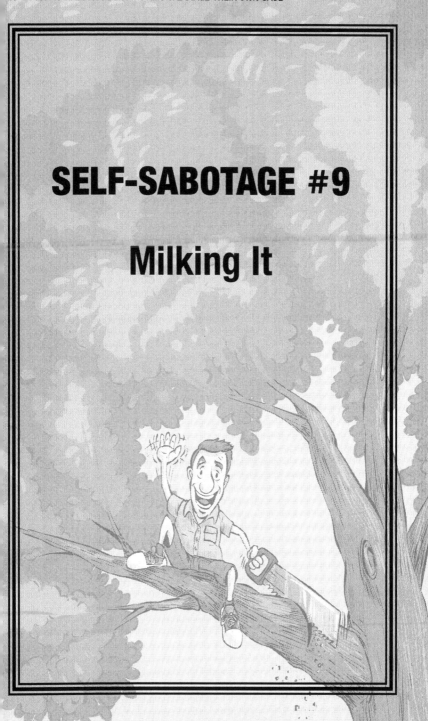

SELF-SABOTAGE #9

Milking It

Milking it for all it's worth.

This is a fantastic way to sabotage your case. A handful of people, for whatever reason, think that exaggerating how serious their injuries are will help them get more money. I'll call them the "milkers," because they attempt to take advantage of the situation and "milk it for all it's worth." On second thought, you just go ahead and call them whatever you want (and please, feel free to be creative!).

Here's what "milkers" do: After they've been hurt in an accident, a stupid idea pops into their head that says "Hey, I can make some easy money here! All I have to do is pretend my injuries are worse than what they really are, and insurance will have to pay me more! Heck, if I'm sneaky enough, who could possibly find out?! This is genius!"

Idiots. First of all, and I know I'm preaching to the choir here, it's dishonest. The point of a personal injury claim is not to win some sort of lottery, but to restore what's been wrongfully taken from you.

Second, what "milkers" don't realize is that eventually, people get suspicious. When they get suspicious, they look with more scrutiny. When they look with more scrutiny, chances are good they're going to find out if the injury victim has been untruthful. If they find out the victim has been untruthful, the jig is up, and the victim will walk away with nothing.

I once had a client where, after a while, I believed less and less of what he said. Things just didn't add up. His doctor picked up on this too. After getting my hands on the client's medical records, I read the words "I don't believe him." Can you guess how much that client ended up getting? That's right – *Nothing*. If not even a person's own doctor believes what he's saying, nobody else is going to either.

Another reason why it's a really bad idea to "milk it" is that insurance companies are naturally paranoid. They go through a great deal to make sure they aren't being scammed. Quite often, they'll hire a private investigator to follow a person around town who has filed an accident-injury claim. And if that person has previously said "My injuries are so bad I can barely walk," but the investigator records footage of him going to the gym, taking long walks with the dog, or carrying a bunch of heavy grocery bags, things are going to get ugly. This won't just wreck his case. No, that will be the least of his worries. The big problem is the insurance company could then take that evidence and file an allegation of insurance fraud. That's a world of hurt you don't want to find yourself in.

I'm not going to sugarcoat things here. "Milkers" have made things a lot harder for you. Because of them, people have become generally distrustful of personal injury victims and their attorneys. They are the stereotype, despite the fact that they only represent a small fraction of the group. This has caused countless jury members to think

"Well, I've heard that most personal injury victims are liars, so this person is probably lying too. Therefore, I'm not going to give them anything." It isn't right or fair, but it's the reality.

I know you already know this, and it goes without saying, but the best way to cut through this ignorant skepticism is to be 100% honest about everything. People are far more likely to believe what is said if it's the truth. So if something hurts a lot, tell your doctor that it hurts a lot. If something only hurts a little, tell your doctor it only hurts a little. And if something doesn't hurt at all, don't tell your doctor that it does. It's as easy as that.

SELF-SABOTAGE #10

Waiting Too Long

Lady Justice hates a messy fridge.

Just like the food in your refrigerator, your case has an expiration date on it. ***In Oregon, the statute of limitations for personal injury claims is two years.*** That means you have to settle your case with the insurance company, or take it to court, within two years of your accident. If you wait too long and your case expires, the law will treat your case like sour milk and, quite literally, toss it in the trash.

The law does this for several reasons. Memories fade, evidence gets lost or destroyed, and there's a greater chance for stories to be fabricated if too much time is allowed to pass by. That's why the law prefers people to resolve their issues relatively quickly, while things are still fresh in their minds and evidence is easily accessible.

Some injury victims prefer to wait until the last minute. They procrastinate until their case is about to expire (nearly two years after their accident) before asking an attorney "Will you take my case?" What they don't realize is that this is like asking a single carpenter "Can you finish building me a house in two weeks?" Sure, I suppose it would be possible to build a house in two weeks. But good luck finding a carpenter who would take the job. Even if you did, would you really want to live in such a hastily built house anyway?

The same goes for a personal injury case. If you waited to see an attorney until your case had nearly expired, sure, I suppose it would be *possible* for an attorney to get everything done before the deadline. But good luck finding an attorney who would take the case. The magnitude of work that would have to get done in such a short amount of time would be enough to drive even the super lawyers to their knees. Even if you did find a willing attorney at the last minute, there would be a greater chance that he or she might miss an important detail that could really hurt your case. So if you decide that you need an attorney, you should start searching for one now. That way there will be plenty of attorneys willing to take your case because they'd have adequate time to do a good job.

There is another very important thing I need to mention. ***In Oregon, if your injuries were caused by a government entity, you or your attorney must notify that entity of your claim against it within 180 days of the accident.*** If you don't, your case will expire and be thrown in the trash. Personally, I think this law is grossly unfair. Many people who would otherwise be entitled to some form of relief are denied simply because they didn't know about a short and harsh deadline. Unfortunately, it doesn't matter what I think. The law is the law, no matter how unbending and unforgiving it can be at times. To make sure this doesn't happen to you, you should speak with an attorney immediately if you were hurt due to the government's negligence.

One More Thing...

If you're like me, you might be thinking "Ok, Mr. Johnstun. You've given me all these tips and pointers, but why should I trust you? Why should I believe that you're looking out for my best interests and not just your own?" These are fair questions. Besides, I was the one who recommended a healthy dose of skepticism in the first place! It's only right that you direct some of that skepticism towards me.

There are at least three different ways I could answer you. First, I could explain how attorneys have a sworn duty of loyalty to their clients so that the interests of the client always come first. Yawn! You know as well as I do that this guarantees nothing. Attorneys are still people, and some people do not take their promises seriously.

The second answer I could give you is the "financially-incentivized" one. With this answer, I would tell you that I have a big incentive to get as much money as I can for you, because I get a percentage of whatever you get. Another way to say this is the more money you get, the more money I get, and so there is no need to worry. I'm not going to give you this answer. We both know that this is no reason to trust somebody. Also, this incentive does not always work. I've seen some personal injury firms who value quantity over quality. They begin by signing up an absurd number of clients. Next, rather than put in the necessary work to get a client everything he or she deserves, they quickly agree to a lower settlement with the insurance company, and put pressure on the client to agree also. Then, the firm will turn around and do the same thing for its next client, and on and on it goes. This enables the firm to make a lot of money by dealing in bulk. Think about it. If a firm is able to settle three cases for 70% of their value in the same time it takes an honest attorney to settle one case for 100% of its value, who's going to make more money? It's not the honest attorney. These sorts of personal injury firms are commonly called "mills," because they treat their clients like commodities, not people.

The third way I could answer would be to tell you personal stories demonstrating how trustworthy I am, but I'm not going to give you this answer either. I respect you enough to know that a few cheap, feel-good paragraphs won't buy your trust. There's just no way around it – trust has to be earned over time, through repeated acts that show one's worthiness of it. All the marketing tricks in the world won't change that. Not for billion-dollar companies, and certainly not for me.

I guess that leaves you without a satisfying answer, doesn't it? Believe me, I wish I could give you one. But as my wife Dawn and I struggled over this question, we realized that there is simply no convincing answer I could give you on paper. We concluded I can't tell you why you should trust me with your case, if you decide you need an attorney. This is something I will have to show you. And that's a bit of a dilemma. Obviously, I can't show you anything unless, at the very least, you ask me about your case. That's a choice you'll have to make on your own. So whatever you choose, I hope you've learned a thing or two by reading this, and I wish you all the best.

Artist's interpretation of the author.

The author running the "Kilted Mile".

A Little About Me

I never planned on being a personal injury attorney. I was aware of the stereotypes surrounding the profession, and I didn't have any intention of being associated with it. I mean, come on, who would want to be called an "ambulance chaser?" Who would want to be viewed by others as some kind of shark who only cares about money? Not me, that's for sure.

For a long time, I didn't know what I wanted to do for a living. All I knew was that whatever it was, it had to provide for my family, and it had to be something where I would get to help people. During my first year of law school, I thought that working as general counsel for a hospital would fulfil those goals for me. I even got an internship at a children hospital's legal department. I loved the fact that in a small way I was helping some of the best doctors in the world perform life-saving miracles on kids.

Believing I had found my calling, I tried to get an internship with another hospital during my second year of law school. I was unsuccessful this time around. I never even got an interview. Not wanting to leave my resume blank for that summer, I decided to apply for positions in other fields. One of those positions was at a personal injury firm. To be perfectly honest, the only reason I applied for it was because I wanted to have a fail-safe, just in case nobody else hired me.

They offered me the job on the spot. Even with absolutely nothing else lined up, I remember saying to my wife "I don't know if I should take this job. It's not even close to the kind of law I want to practice, and I've heard it can get a little shady too." But, agreeing that something was better than nothing, I unenthusiastically took the job.

The attorney who hired me, Dale Pugh, looked in many ways more like a mountain man than a lawyer. He had a gray beard, a horse hide briefcase, and wore cowboy boots and a denim jacket on casual Fridays. His demeanor was often gruff and uninviting. To top things off, Dale was a former Marine and FBI agent who spent his time capturing spies during the Cold War. Frankly, I was intimidated by the man.

Despite his hard shell, it didn't take me long to figure out that Dale was one of the most generous people I'd ever met. I saw plenty of injured people come to him who had seen at least five other attorneys, and every one of those attorneys had turned them down. It wasn't that these people had frivolous claims or anything. Other attorneys just saw these claims as requiring too much work for too little pay. Dale, however, signed these people up all the time, knowing full well it wasn't the business-savvy thing to do. I watched him pour hundreds of hours into cases like this. When I asked him why, he said "If I don't take care of these people, nobody else will."

It was Dale who helped me realize I had been grossly misinformed about personal injury law. It wasn't from anything he said, because he hardly said anything to me at first (unless I got him talking about his FBI stories). I learned through simple observation. His clients weren't a bunch of people looking to cheat the system and get rich quick, like society would have us believe. What I saw instead was legitimately, and often times tragically, hurt people who only wanted enough money to get back on their feet but were being ignored by the insurance company. Without somebody like Dale who was skilled at his profession and willing to work on the cheap, these people would have continued to be ignored, and they never would have seen any justice for the harm that had been done to them. That's when I decided to become a personal injury attorney, and I haven't looked back since.

Johnstun Injury Law
P.O. Box 1660
St. Helens, OR 97051
Phone: (503)610-5399
Fax: (866)955-2236
johnstun.injury.law@outlook.com